W9-BWD-926

THE WORLD OF GEORGE PRICE

THE WORLD OF GEORGE PRICE

A 55-YEAR RETROSPECTIVE

Introduced by Alistair Cooke

A Peter Weed Book
BEAUFORT BOOKS PUBLISHERS
New York

Also by George Price

MY DEAR 500 FRIENDS
GEORGE PRICE'S CHARACTERS
THE PEOPLE ZOO
ICE COLD WAR
IS IT ANYONE WE KNOW?
WE BUY OLD GOLD
WHO'S IN CHARGE HERE?
IT'S SMART TO BE PEOPLE
GOOD HUMOR MAN
BROWSE AT YOUR OWN RISK

Copyright © 1988 by George Price

Library of Congress Catalog Number: 87-24134

ISBN 0-8253-0449-0

Of the 363 drawings in this book, 324 appeared
originally in *The New Yorker* and were copyrighted ©
in the years 1931–1988, inclusive, by The New Yorker
Magazine, Inc. Twelve drawings are appearing here
for the first time.

Published in the United States of America by
Beaufort Books Publishers, New York

All Rights Reserved
Printed in the United States of America
First Edition

To the memory of
John Corcoran

George Price on Marriage and Other Disasters

by Alistair Cooke

In the summer of 1979, Jimmy Carter took the *Delta Queen* down the Mississippi and revealed to the riverbank crowds, at all hours of the day and night, a toothy figure in T-shirt, jeans, and sneakers to enforce the reminder that the President of the United States was Jimmy Carter still, a humble Georgia farmer closer to the people than the populist upstart from Beverly Hills. The White House reckoned without the *Chicago Tribune*'s MacNelly, who produced a cartoon of a Mississippi riverboat bearing down at full cock on a raft carrying, in silhouette, Carter as Huck Finn and Mondale as Nigger Jim. Carter is shouting: "Nobody here but me and ma man Jim"—*(sotto voce)* "Shuffle a little, Jim." Ole Jim hisses back: "I cain't, ah'd scuff ma Guccis."

It was a more vivid memento of a brave, if half-baked, enterprise than the cruise itself. Like popular verse in the nineteenth century—like "The Charge of the Light Brigade" and "The Midnight Ride of Paul Revere"— the MacNelly version was the one that would stick. At any rate, it was a lively reminder that since the disappearance of popular poetry as a medium of political pleading, the political cartoonists—in this country, MacNelly, Oliphant, Conrad, Herblock—have become Shelley's "unacknowledged legislators of the world." It would be too much to say that Herblock destroyed Nixon, but his unshaven figure skulking always along the gutter impressed on the popular imagination a stereotype which prejudiced the outcome of Watergate even before the Senate hearings had begun.

The New Yorker has not been renowned for political cartoonists. Perhaps because it was founded at a time when its likely contributors, the intelligent young brought up on Mencken's *American Mercury*, took on the fashionable contempt for all politicians and directed their rebellion, in gentler ways, at the crasser symbols of the Coolidge prosperity: the sugar daddy, the bonehead debutante, pretentious suburbanites, muscle-bound athletes, women's clubs, Park Avenue tycoons, big-game hunters, bathing beauties. Doddering clubmen deploring Roosevelt were about as far as it went by way of a political statement. *The New Yorker* had no political line, but whether knowingly or not it was a creation of non-card-carrying liberal Democrats and, to a greater than lesser extent, still is.

Alongside the objects of its ridicule were set the compensating objects of its sympathy at the other end of the social scale: Steig's small fry, shrewd barflies, comic beggars, wistful window-shoppers, philosophical jailbirds, and Whitney Darrow's world of innocent secretaries, amiably befuddled wives, dog lovers, and affable cocktail buffoons.

Into this stable of greatly gifted artists burst, fifty-five years ago, a man who could never be described as a liberal Democrat. He was George Price, a born anarchist who, with different origins, might have led the revolution as a latter-day Nast, if his upbringing had not thrown him in with a cast of characters whose comicality impressed him more than their social plight. His father was a set builder for silent movies, his mother toiled away at a sewing machine. As a boy, he must have picked up from them and their workmates his precise and funny knowledge of building materials and household gadgetry. (In old age, he told Charles Addams: "No plumber has ever criticized my drawings.")

He was born in New Jersey, "at the end of a trolley line," and was at once exposed to arrivals from Hackensack and Jersey City—Irish, Germans, Italians—who were firemen, carpenters, saloon keepers, dog track habitués, delicatessen owners, hausfrauen with many children ("all of whom had heads about the size of my fist"). These were his people, observed and enjoyed with a total lack of sentimentality or condescending pity. He marveled at their dumb ingenuity, their mad energy or affable sloth, their offhand fatalism before broken pumps or terminally ill husbands. And these were the people he drew, in the early days, for *The New Yorker*.

His style was not then easily recognizable. It was a rapid, seemingly carefree, sinuous style, but the litheness the figures aimed at was marred by excessive shading and many creases in the clothing that belied the anatomy underneath. In short, it was not a personal style at all but an amalgam of several hesitant styles derived from the old *Life* and *Judge*. I can say this without fear of protest even from the man himself, for he has dismissed the draftsmanship of those early years as "pretty awful."

At some point, the shading began to diminish, the creases were reduced to the posture of the body itself. You can see from this collection how gradually, but how firmly, these changes took place. By the mid-1940s at the latest, the George Price we can spot—and revere—at thirty feet has arrived. (Compare his drawing of the cops in "He never knew what hit him"—June 29, 1935— with that of the money-lender of April 27, 1946.) And for the past forty years, we have had one of the half-dozen *New Yorker* artists who are instantly

"He never knew what hit him."

recognizable for wholly original styles. Indeed, the wonder of Price's draftsmanship is the demonstrable fact that the boldness, the absolute inevitability,
of his line has grown through his seventies and eighties.

He once said—I think with remarkable generosity—that everybody in the
New Yorker group had improved in draftsmanship down the years, a judgment
I should be inclined to challenge if it is taken to include a more recent crop
of cartoonists who seem to have learned to draw with a straw, or with their
elbows, and always will. But it is truer of Price than of any in the *New Yorker*
stable, even of the other great ones.

At some point, too, not—I should guess—before his middle age, he
discarded the Hackensack circus of odd characters and made a vow to "take
a crack at all the joiners—the Ku Klux Klan, the rednecks, those clucks who
belong to all the fraternal organizations . . . I despise all these 'America—
love it or leave it' types. I'm not anti-anything, except anti-muttonhead."
The muttonheads are not hard to identify. Later still, about a quarter-
century ago, he came to concentrate on the soured couple in the kitchen
(surprising how many *New Yorker* cartoons are about failed marriages). He
became the inventor and sole proprietor of the raddled wife and her bulbous,
cross-eyed mate torpid before the TV—resigned to the marital truce. Their
milieu, Israel Shenker has written, is "lumpenproletariat hodgepodge."

Bernard Shaw said of Mark Twain that if his adoring readers had sensed
the deadly seriousness of the things he was funny about, they would have
lynched him. Price is more cunning still. The sublime clownishness of his
two main characters provides a purge for all nagging couples ("Things may
be bad in our house, but never that bad") and hides the fact that what we are
looking at is a Hackensack Willy Loman. Otherwise, this book could be
entitled "George Price: A Chronicle of Appalling Marriages."

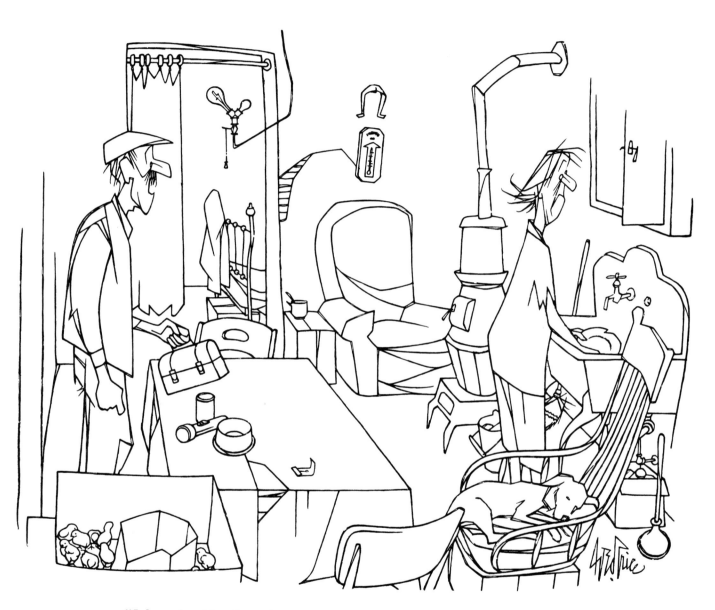

"I heard a bit of good news today. We shall pass this way but once."

*"Fifth floor—crockery, chinaware, kitchen utensils
and a mysterious little room marked 'No Admittance'!"*

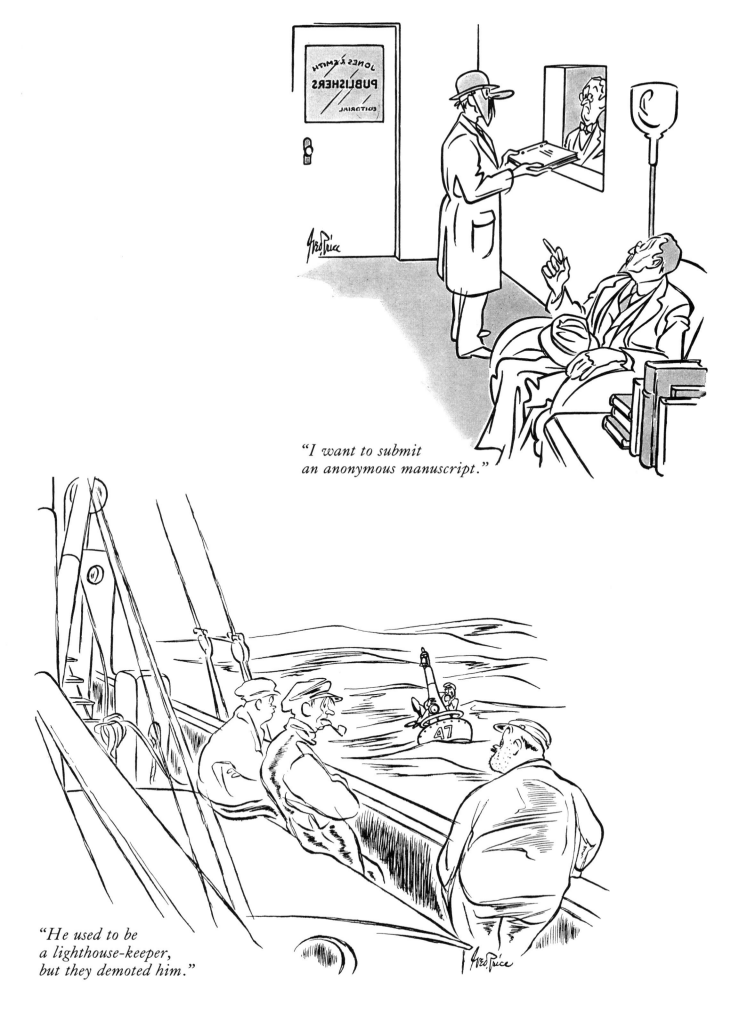

"I want to submit
an anonymous manuscript."

"He used to be
a lighthouse-keeper,
but they demoted him."

"Oh, it's you. I *thought* I heard the rustle of silk."

"That's right, stupid—drop 'em all over the lot!"

"It's just the river—it comes up this way every year."

"But the Taj Mahal was ticky-tacky, I thought."

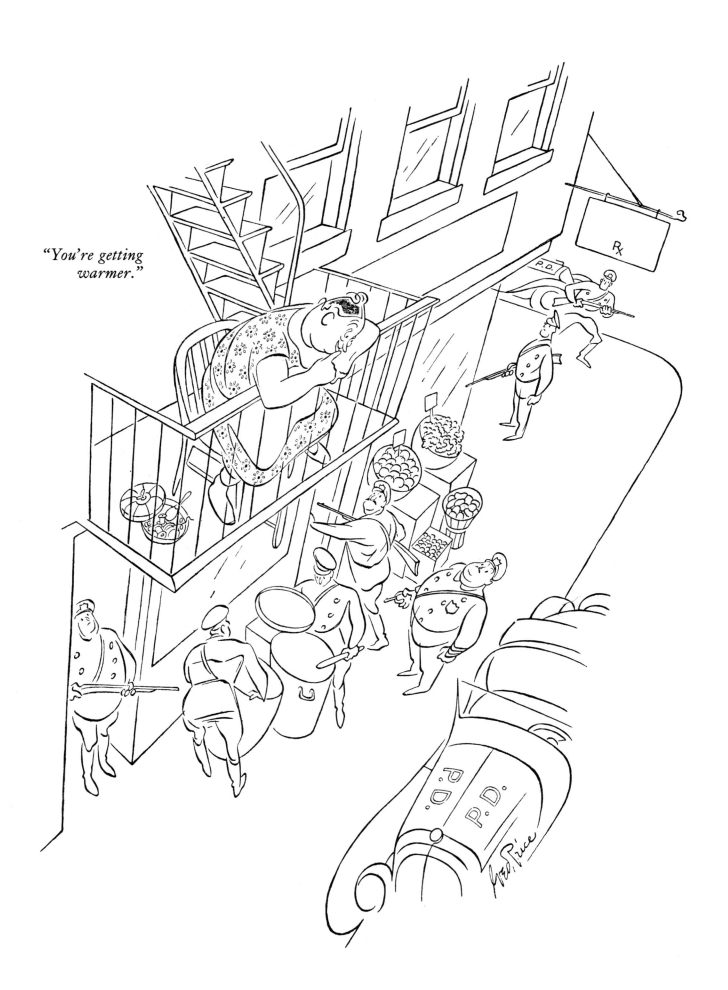

"You're getting warmer."

"*Money is his god.*"

"Mind if I smoke?"

"He didn't really die of anything. He was a hypochrondriac."

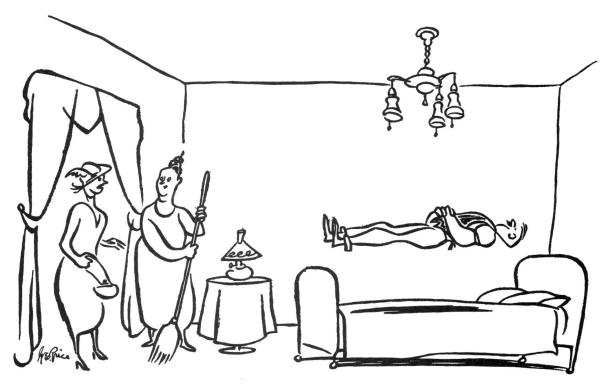

"He's been up a week now, and there's nothin' we can do about it."

"*They couldn't rent this booth. It's haunted by the ghost of an old Pope-Toledo.*"

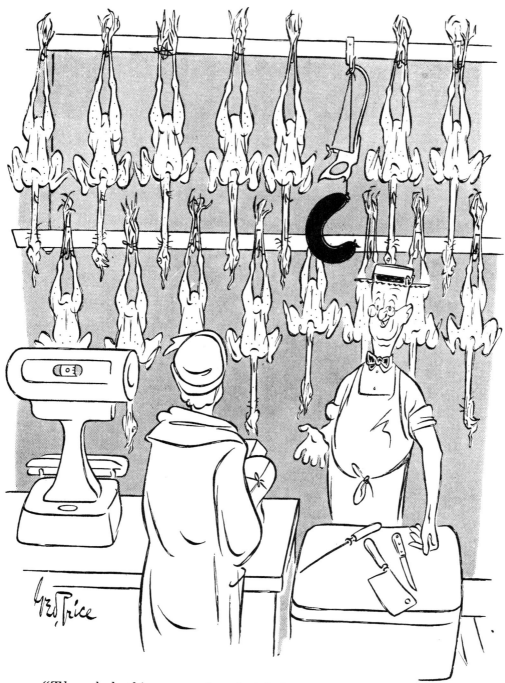

"The whole thing seemed to shriek for just one comic effect."

"Harry wasn't born great and he hasn't achieved greatness, but he figures there is always the chance that greatness may be thrust upon him."

"Thank you. You're aging gracefully yourself."

"He's beginning to sit up now and take nourishment."

"*. . . and a right and a left, and
another left, and a jolting right to the head . . .*"

"I don't know what it is. I shot it one time when I had jungle fever."

"Peyton should go far—if he doesn't crack."

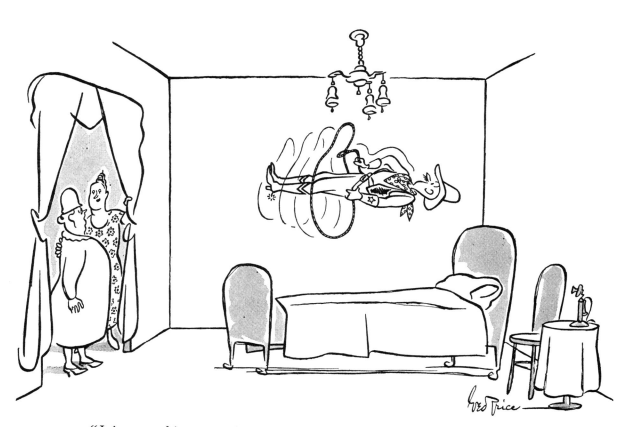

"I just got him a cowboy suit. Sit down and watch him a while."

"*And I am well aware of the fact that to be here many of you travelled considerable distances in inclement weather. Therefore, I will get directly to the point.*"

"I got in late—mind if I see how it started?"

"About your mother's stiff neck. Tell her I cried 'Alas!'"

"Put out your light, dear, and come to bed."

*"The moon has something to do
with it. Lately he's been rising and falling with the tide."*

"O.K., gang. Let's hear it for Mr. Kirby."

"I think he does it with mirrors, but whatever it is — it's damned unsettling!"

"Libra (September 23-October 23): Busy, busy, busy. The accent is on excitement and romance. Be ready for a flurry of calls, invitations . . ."

"'Pack up your troubles in your old kit bag and smile, smile, smile.'"

"He never knew what hit him."

"If you were down here, you'd damn well know why I keep saying 'we.'"

*"And what's the rap
if I don't <u>choose</u> to pay the fine?"*

"I'll miss you. 'Mary' is a grand old name."

"You know how it is. You have a little more, you live a little better."

"I'm a boy."

"Sure there's something you can do. You can lay out the place cards."

"*Why, this appears to be the same thing in a cheap papyrus edition.*"

"And don't disturb his naps. When you wake him, he's an absolute fountain of platitudes."

"B.K. Howley here—cordless."

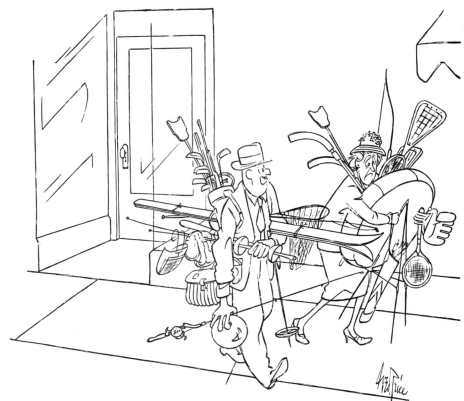

"Certainly they cost a lot of money, but it's time we started getting some fun out of life!"

"Oh, dear! And we didn't get anything for him!"

"Face the front of the car, please!"

"Maybe we'd better cut down a little on the plant food."

"*Poor Father doesn't know what to do with himself since he's retired.*"

"Mind if I eat this here?"

"He calls it the cultivation of serenity. I call it just plain laziness."

"*Is this cabin pressurized properly? My baked apple just blew up.*"

"*Can you give me a run down on the dramatis personae?*"

"Thought our luck seemed a little exceptional, Gibson."

*"Quit saying 'In all my seventeen years of refereeing'
and start counting him out!"*

"I'll see what the rule book says about it."

"Say, Jackson, here's something curious."

"I understand they're a ménage à trois."

"Forty-five cents a pound—as is."

"Oh, for heaven's sake! <u>Watch</u> 'The Dukes of Hazard'!"

"You've got a nice act there, Fredricson, but I think you're just asking for trouble with the musicians' union."

"Don't ask _me_. He leads his life and I lead mine."

"That's a rather poor start at a shoplifting career, Madam."

"What he needs is a change of scene. Why don't you move him to some other window?"

"Lord, how you must have suffered!"

"*And this is our breakfast nook, where the dawns come up like thunder.*"

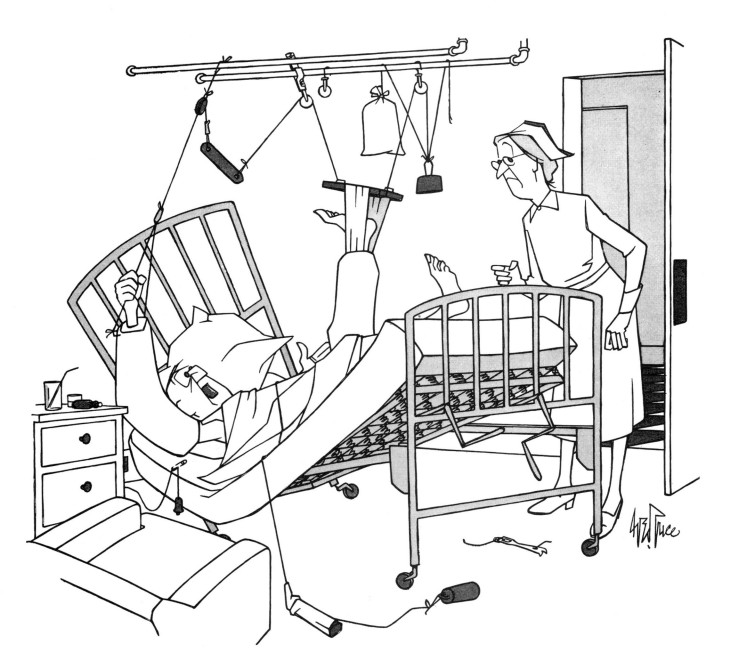

"*Something suddenly just went BOING!*"

"I don't care <u>who</u> started it."

"Don't fall for it. It's what they call psychology."

"You have the wrong number,
but even if you had the right number I'm
sure he'd have no statement for the press."

"I.R.T.? I want to report a leak."

"This must be the last family bar in the Bronx."

"Did you telephone for a sitter?"

DEPT. OF
SANITATION
1922

"We must have made a wrong turn somewhere."

"Now get one more, for Aunt Minnie's room."

"No, he isn't."

"It's Day One of the merry month of May. You want a piece of the action?"

"And, what's more, just any old
bird won't do. It's got to be a Baltimore oriole."

"He's homesick."

"O.K., but just one bong and out you both go."

"Ralph! Do we need money?"

"He's one of those people who need people."

"Farewell, brave lover! Come back either with your shield or upon it."

"Here comes Dolan now!"

"*Nathaniel's expecting his Civil War Book Club selection today.*"

"*Erskine, you know that different drummer you're always marching to?*"

"True. But what it says about him is something I've known for years."

"After I've tried every known system, she's breaking the bank with that silly ibbity-bibbity-sibbity-sab stuff!"

"Your mother is a very remarkable woman, Herbert."

"Whew! 'Tain't a fit night out for man nor beast!"

"*For the last time, open up or we'll smash the door down!*"

"Thank you, Paine Webber."

"I understand there's a little comedy relief in the second act."

"I'll be at Georgette's Laundromat and Bar-and-Grill."

"Al Disbrow? I believe he went into the V.I.P. Lounge."

"The house does wonderful on that one."

*"A powerful glass, sir. Looks like I'm right
on top of you, doesn't it?"*

"Edward has an Aunt Fiona who is neither fish nor fowl, haven't you, dear?"

"Lots of new faces this year."

"*What better way to say Merry Christmas?*"

"Hey, Martha! Guess what!"

"About four months ago, he had a room added to the house,
and I haven't laid eyes on him since."

"When you drive, I lock up. When I drive, you lock up. Right?"

"All right, boys—break it up!"

"*Good night, and thanks for allowing us into your living room.*"

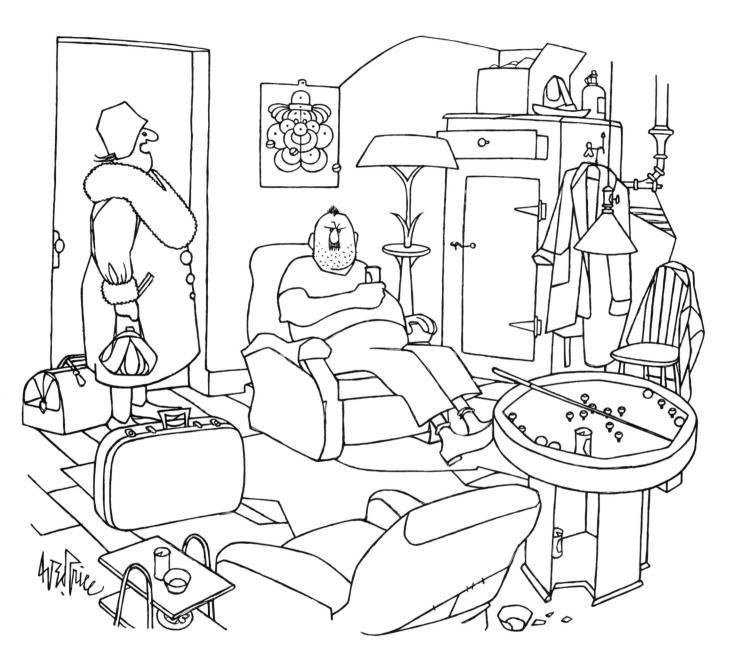

"Le Car keys, s'il vous plaît!"

"We don't sell them singly, Madam. It breaks up the formation."

"Watch out, Fred! Here it comes again!"

"Well, she has her books and I have my dogs."

"Lord, what a day!"

"So! You've devoured your mate. Well,
good for *you*, Olga, honey."

"I'm sorry, Gilhorn, but J.W. himself has decided you are
no longer bright-eyed and bushy-tailed."

"*Hey, pal! Care to hire an entourage?*"

"Oven-ready costs a few cents more and oven-ready is worth a few cents more!"

"*He came at me like this but conked himself instead. He never was handy with tools.*"

"Well, so far his behavior has been exemplary."

"Mr. and Mrs. Herman L. Lembaugh, of 435 Grand Concourse, the Bronx, offer their only daughter, Ethel, to the winner of the five-lap sprint."

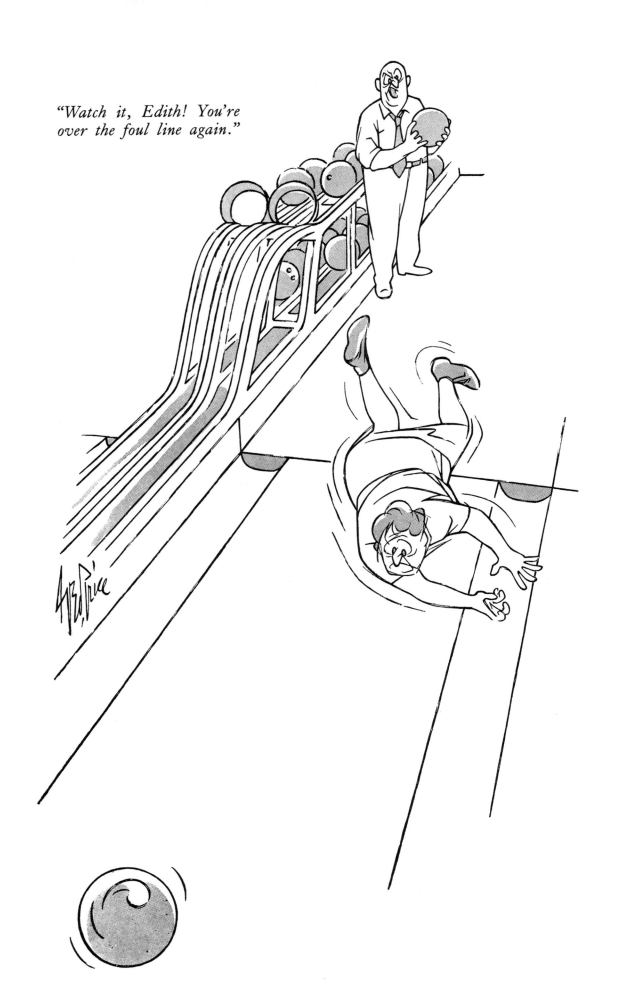

"Watch it, Edith! You're over the foul line again."

"And as a consequence the silver-bell tinkle has gone out of my laughter."

"In non-technical language, Mrs. Wilson, it's busted."

"Agnes, I'm trying to come up with a Sunday sermon. Do you suppose you could be all sweetness and light in another part of the house?"

"For the last time,
I'm asking you to take down that Christmas tree."

"All in all, folks, it's quite an inning."

"Howdy, stranger!"

"Well, shall we get on with our golden years?"

"It won't be long now, sir. The kitchen is a beehive of activity."

"Where did we go wrong?"

"*I can't get a peep out of him.
You sure he went down the tube?*"

"*They all look promising enough, but I wish we had greater diversity.*"

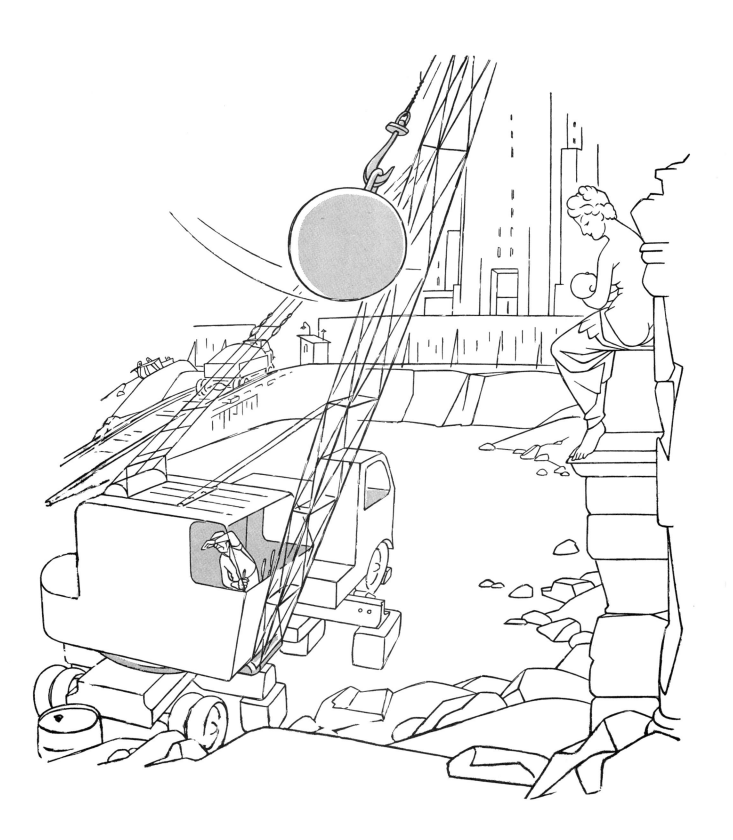

"Now the game begins to make some sense!"

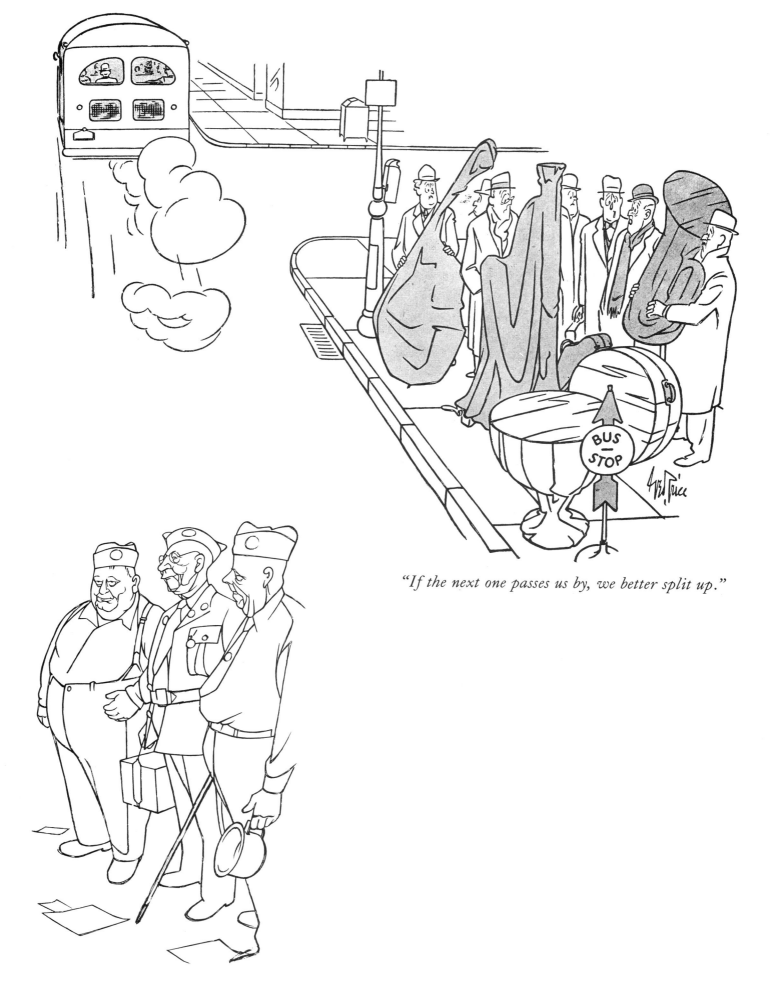

"If the next one passes us by, we better split up."

"It's some odd-ball salesman."

"Don't ask __me__ which fork. __You__ bought the sweepstakes ticket."

"*Or in the language of a layman, Mr. Hyde,*
you're hungry. What you need is something to eat."

"*Play 'Misty' for me.*"

"Just Molly and me, and baby makes three . . ."

"Careful, darling. You're not as young as you used to be."

"Ding! Dong! Your toast is done, through the courtesy of the Citizens' National Bank, which pays six per cent on Investor's Passbook accounts."

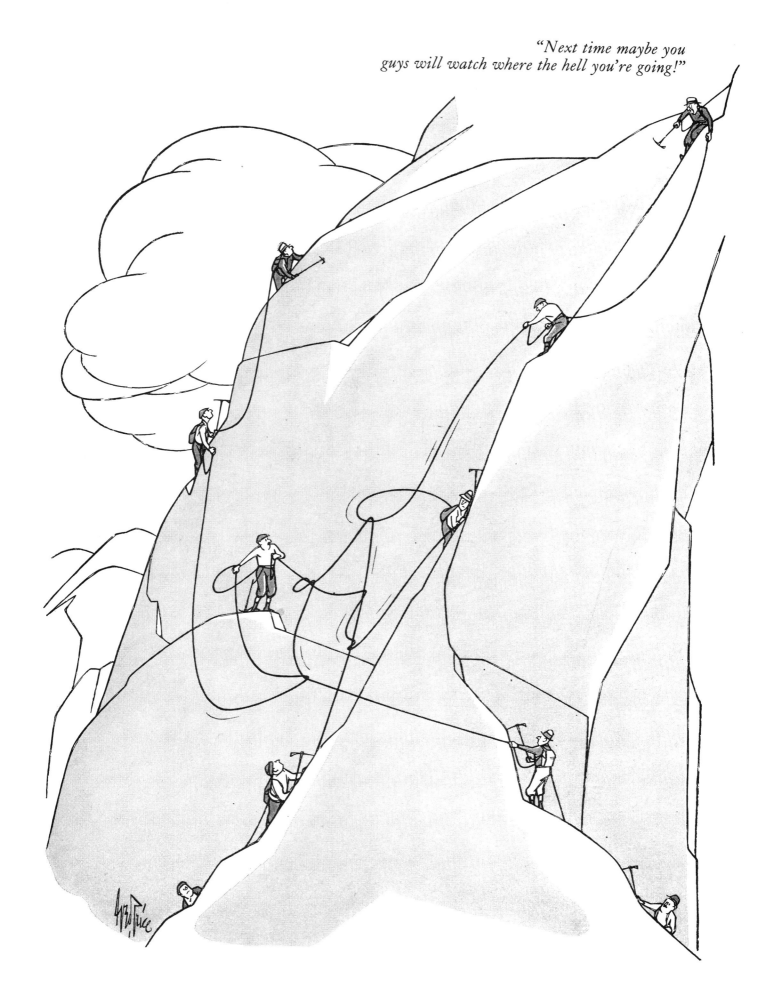

"Next time maybe you guys will watch where the hell you're going!"

"Welcome to Expo 07."

"Sorry, folks. The chef just threw in the towel on the boiled tripe à la Grecque."

"Twelve, please!"

"It's the last pair of yellow button shoes in the store—and they both want them!"

"It says 'Please turn to page 14.' Hah! That'll be the day."

"I'll be hoisting a few down at Grogan's. You keep the conversational ball rolling."

"Maybe I just haven't suffered enough. Why don't you whip up some of
your curried pork balls and refried rice for dinner?"

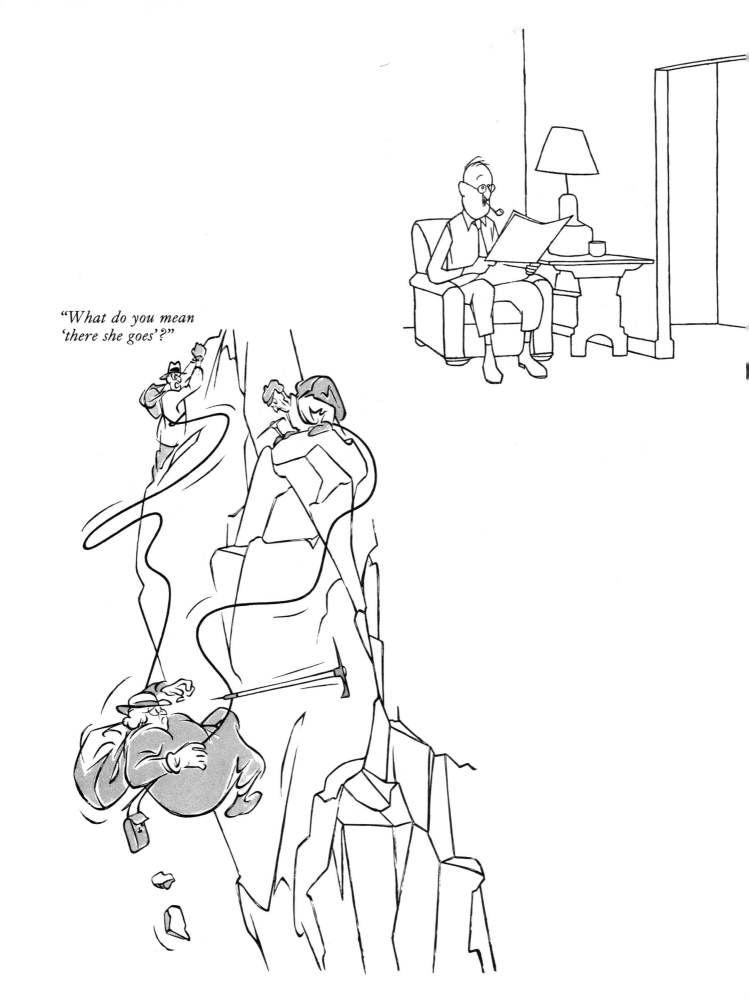

"Is there no end to your treachery?"

"I've told him there's nothing doing, but they just keep sitting there."

"I'm putting all my money into 'things.'"

"Who made up this guest list—Norman Lear?"

"Hmmm — you know something, Charlie?"

"Then in 1927, against Clinton High, with only two minutes to play . . ."

"I don't know why I should have such a headache. I do a strictly cash business."

"It's a no-pepperoni pizza—a message of hope for all mankind."

"Here's the guest room. Just make yourselves at home."

"Could we come back tomorrow? We're still two for, two against, and one undecided."

"Was Mommy gone long?"

"Aloha! Aloha from the bottom of my heart."

"Lift your stems."

"Will you please listen to <u>me</u> for a minute?"

"But don't expect too much. Carl hasn't touched his kazoo in years."

"*What kind of book have you written?*"

"I did not say it wasn't a super-shot. I merely said that I, personally, was not electrified."

"*You keep parading around in that wetsuit, but you never get wet.*"

"Would there be a bosky dell hereabouts?"

"This will give you a rough idea of how it will look."

"He likes the patter of tiny feet."

From the desk of Vladimir Bronsk

"*Just spending another evening in the bosom of my family. What are you doing?*"

"I'd like my husband to see it first."

"I'll be on the main drag, turning a few heads."

"It suddenly occurred to me today that it's been exactly
nine years since you liked my attitude."

"Just drive straight ahead, sir. We'll have you out of here in a jiffy."

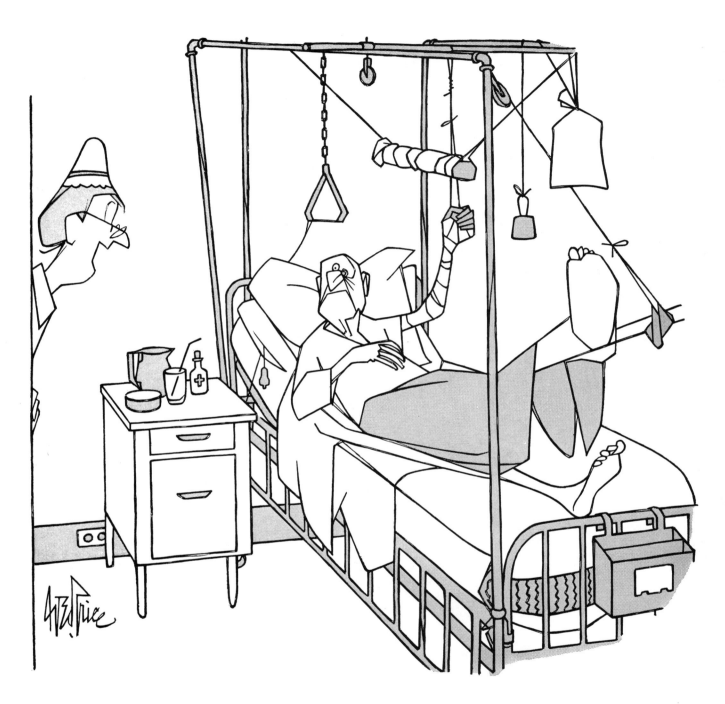

"*Have your pillows been plumped this morning?*"

"That's what several other people have said."

"His sermon last Sunday, 'The Meek Shall Inherit the Earth,' had them rolling in the aisles."

"I'll have a nice day when
I get damn good and ready."

"Good morning, sir. Do you feel unappreciated? Neglected? Lacking
in recognition for something you've done?"

"Having the whitest wash on the block, week after week — surely there must be more to life than that."

"I wonder would you be good enough, the next time you get your adrenalin flowing, to bring me a glass of iced tea."

"Where do I <u>always</u> go when the whippoorwills call and evening is nigh? To Large Lena's Kaboom Room."

"*Ed's always been a good provider.*"

"Right in the middle of Lawrence Welk, he stood up, said, 'Toot, Toot, Tootsie, Goodbye,' and I haven't seen him since."

"Instill in him a fine sense of humor and to hell with all the rest of it."

"Ah! The eye of the storm, I presume."

"The one that cottons up to me, I'll take."

"You were right. It's the conniptions."

"*These days, everybody is looking for answers.*"

"Is it anyone we know?"

"So *that's* where the door is!"

"Ah, the iceman cometh."

"I'll be in the parlor, eating bread and honey."

"Well, I'll say good night. Emmett wants to go home."

"I must admit
I envy his philosophy."

"To you and yours."

"*Did you see a walking sprinkler go by here?*"

"*It all goes in the home-entertainment center.*"

"*I never promised you a rose garden.*"

*"If it's a Liberty nickel, 1913,
I'll be able to pay you right away, Doc."*

"And then, having shaped up, he shipped out."

"Remember now, _you_ got the brains."

"Which way to the House of Good Taste, Mac?"

"I believe I'll take the baked-meatloaf trip."

*"For goodness' sake, can't I raise the teeniest objection to our foreign
policy without you waving the flag in my face?"*

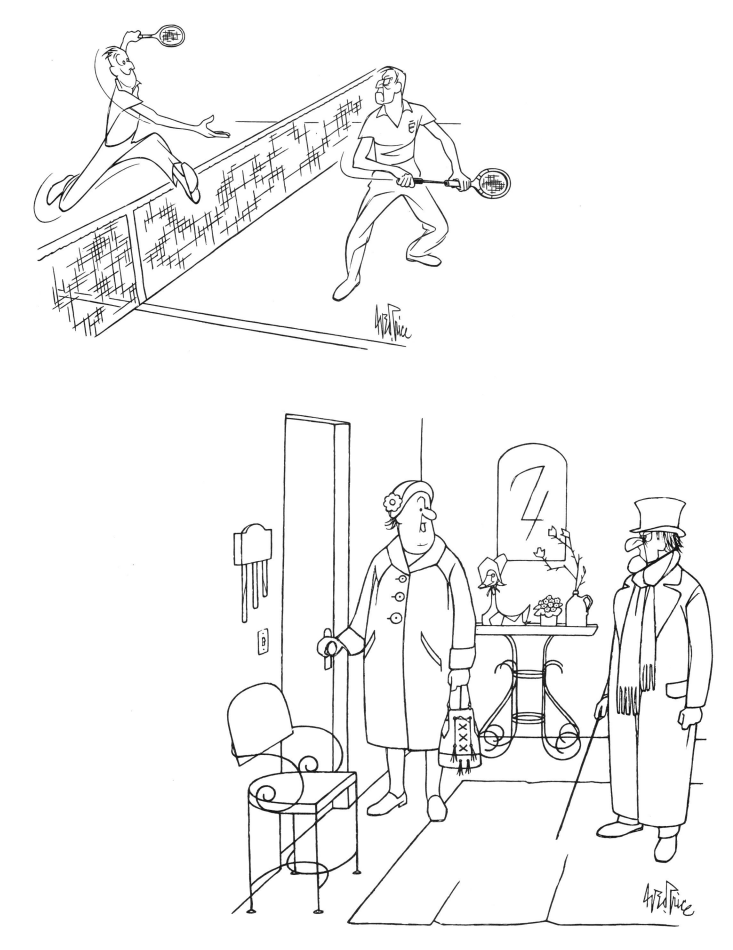

"*Aren't you a bit early with the holiday spirit?*"

*"Twelve years you studied in Vienna, doctor,
and all you can advise is scattering peanut shells?"*

"We were a party of four, if you don't mind!"

"Let's go, Mets!"

"Bon appétit."

"Is it my fault they weren't all Grade A Large?"

"I didn't say God is dead. I simply said that my hubcaps were lifted while I attended church."

"When *I* fly, Miss, I *dress* for flying."

"Somewhere, I can't help thinking, there's a load of buckshot with my name on it."

"The tumult and the shouting dies; The captains and the kings depart."

" 'Loving Each Other.' "

"Stop acting so innocent,
Craddock! You know very well _what_ signals."

*"I did shout for help, but the
tide of battle suddenly changed in my favor, thank you."*

"It's Tuesday. Act I, Scene 1."

"*We now return you to your local studios—and good riddance.*"

"To be repaid in full in twelve months. We're not interested in lifelong friendships."

"The chill factor, as I make it, is $3,776.83."

"To your brother. And, this being the Year of the Rat, to rodents everywhere."

"No one but a heathen would rotate his tires at a drive-in-church."

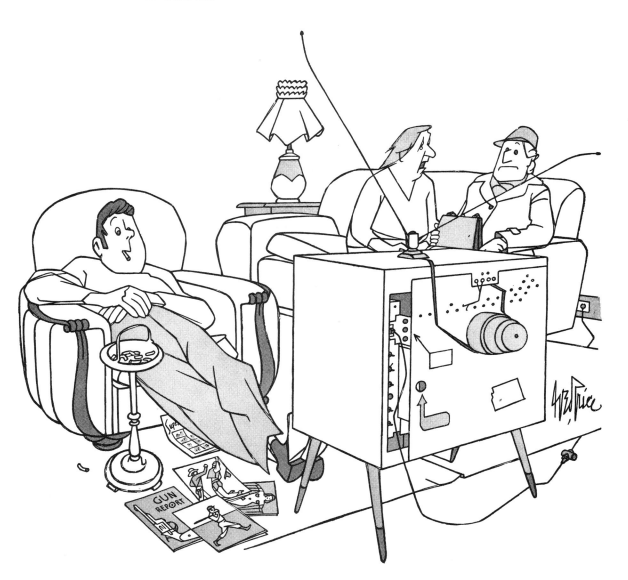

"Success came too early. When he was ten, he hit three homers in three times up in the Little League, and nothing has seemed worth while since."

"I figured you were home. My soufflé just fell."

"When hootenanny beckons us, we're ready."

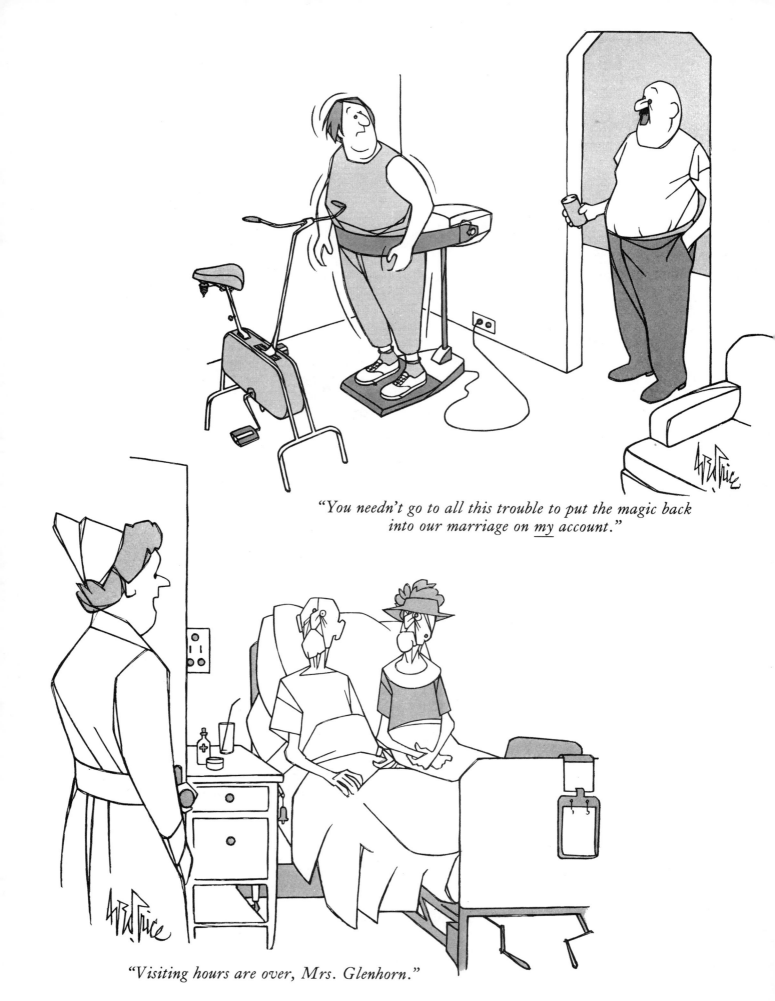

"You needn't go to all this trouble to put the magic back
into our marriage on *my* account."

"Visiting hours are over, Mrs. Glenhorn."

"In short, a ménage à trois is not for every Tom, Dick, and Harriet."

"This weekend, I thought I'd pop over to Vegas and grab a smoke."

"You were right, honey. It *is* too good for the likes of me."

"*Try to forgive me. I'm afraid I haven't been very good company for the past forty-six years.*"

"*I'll be on the porch, pushing ninety.*"

"*For dessert, we have Twinkies, Hostess cupcakes, or Devil Dogs.*"

"Surf's up!"

"*I'll be in the back yard, writing love letters in the sand.*"

"Your mother's up and about. I hear castanets."

"To begin with, you were a dog in the manger _last_ year."

"The italics, I assume, are yours."

"Oh, stop griping! We're fulfilling a lifelong dream, aren't we?"

"*Madam, please! What I distinctly said was that I could lick any <u>man</u> in the house.*"

"It's taken her thirty-one years, but, by God, she's got our marriage working again."

"Were there any important messages for the men in the audience while I was out?"

"You'll note the cross-ventilation."

"*Just between you and me, I'm beginning to rue the day she emerged from her cocoon.*"

"Edna tells me we haven't been seeing enough of you folks,
but I don't buy that."

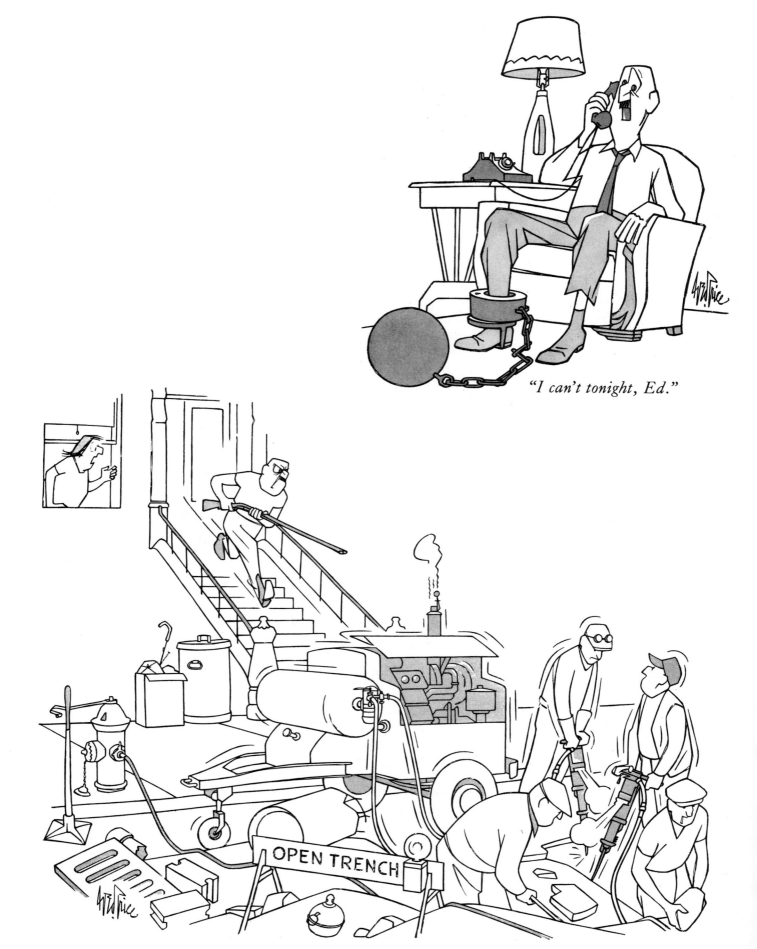

"I can't tonight, Ed."

"Harry, don't! Dig they must!"

"Very well, cook him!"

"It's Ham Hocks Tuesday—a day that will live in infamy."

"His peak earning years came and went without a ripple."

"I'll be at the Blue Pelican Lounge, storing up nuts for the winter."

"I don't know about your tick bird, but mine's sitting on a bonanza."

"The man I have in mind won't be laying any elephant jokes on me. Are you that man, Mr. Pickering?"

"Look who's going to be 'brief and to the point.'"

"He parlayed that frank, open countenance into a place of honor at the public trough."

"Will you be right home after the peccadillo?"

"Now that you ask, no, I don't believe there is a bottom to my little bag of tricks."

"I have this recurring dream about reclining on a bed of wild rice."

"Any word as to the nature of the soupe du jour?"

"If you shouldn't make it, old girl, I'll tell them back home that you gave it your best."

"I'll be in the den, contemplating the bust of Homer."

"*Now are you convinced that the best is yet to be as you grow old along with me?*"

"*And the strings of my heart haven't gone zing from that day to this.*"

"Well! This looks like an idea whose time has come!"

"Say 'Delighted to meet you.' I'll explain later."

"*Congratulations! Burke's Peerage has traced you back to William the Conqueror!*"

"Ah! The people versus Herman Pretzfelder."

"Do you want beer with your pigs' knuckles, or will you meet them head on?"

"I like the way you wrinkle your nose when you laugh."

*"I'll have the stuffed pepper,
and himself will have the quarter-pounder."*

"It's me, Clara—authorized personnel."

"It's a ham and swiss on rye—one of the all-time greats."

"Are we interested in saving Florida alligators?"

"She's looking at 'Nightwatch,' while I hold back the dawn."

"*The last time I saw him, he was heading across the lawn on his seven-horsepower, thirty-two-inch, heavy-duty Craftsman rotary mower.*"

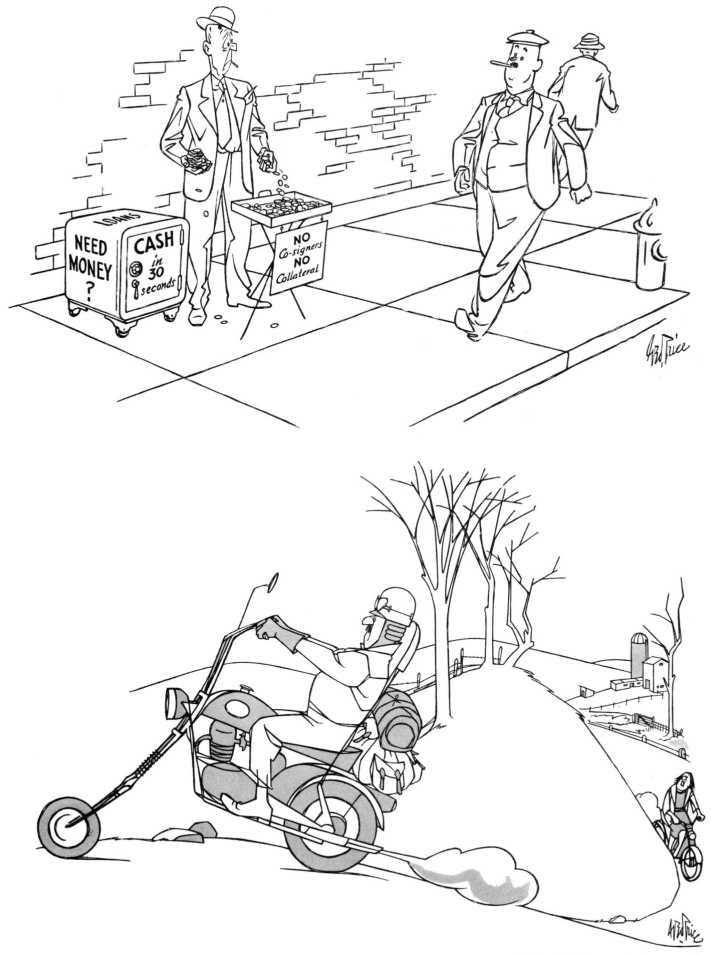

"Wilbur, please come home! The children ask for you."

"*Dinner will be a little late. I spent most of the day counting my blessings.*"

"*Three months we've been here, and <u>still</u> no Welcome Wagon.*"

"What *I* like about that getup is the way his socks fall down every time I clear my throat."

"Could I borrow a little flotsam and jetsam?"

"I tremble every time he gets another one of those crazy catalogues."

"The keeper says for us to get together."

"It's Julia Child's cutlets with Galloping Gourmet sauce."

"Ah, another precinct heard from!"

"At what hour tomorrow do you wish to resume your humdrum existence?"

"Gwen's aunt. She came upon a midnight dreary."

"*I'm sorry, but I'm afraid Mr. Tetlow feels he couldn't live with '114 Pussy Willow Lane' on his personal stationery.*"

"Was it something I averred?"

"I wish we'd never _seen_ Mexico."

"Something in a nice white wine."

"How does cockles and mussels alive, alive-o sound to you?"

"Look, lady, if it's trendy you want, Bloomie's is at Fifty-ninth and Lex."

"Couldn't you just hang me in effigy, as has been your custom?"

"Ah, Indian pudding—the coup de grâce."